SEASONS

Summer

Explore the world with **Popcorn** - your complete first non-fiction library.

Look out for more titles in the **Popcorn** range. All books have the same format of simple text and awesome images. Text is carefully matched to the pictures to help readers to identify and understand key vocabulary. www.waylandbooks.co.uk/popcorn

First published in 2009 by Wayland
First published in paperback in 2011
Copyright © Wayland 2009

Wayland
Hachette Children's Books
338 Euston Road
London NW1 3BH

Wayland Australia
Level 17/207 Kent Street
Sydney NSW 2000

Senior Editor: Claire Shanahan
Designer: Ruth Cowan
Picture Researcher: Louise Edgeworth
Concept Designer: Paul Cherrill

British Library Cataloguing in Publication Data:
Barnham, Kay
Summer. - (Popcorn. Seasons)
1. Summer - Juvenile literature
I. Title
508.2

ISBN: 978 07502 6720 5

Printed and bound in China

Wayland is a division of Hachette Children's Books, an Hachette UK Company.
www.hachette.co.uk

Acknowledgements:
Alamy: Jerome Flynn p4-5, Louise Murray p13, Streetfly Stock , COVER, p17; Corbis: Michael DeYoung p16; Dreamstime.com: Misty Diller Title page, Sofiaworld p8, Antonio Nunes p10, Misty Diller p15; Getty Images: Uwe Krejci/Taxi p7, Stuart Redler/Taxi p9, Ron Sherman/Stone p19; IStockphoto: Nathan McClunie Imprint page, Nathan McClunie p11, Paul Piebinga p14, p18; Naturepl.com: Kim Taylor p12.

Contents

The seasons   4

Summer weather   6

Summer trees   8

Summer flowers   10

Animals in summer   12

Summer food   14

Summer holidays   16

Summer festivals   18

Why do we have seasons?   20

Make a holiday scrapbook   22

Glossary   24

Index   24

The seasons

There are four seasons in the year. The seasons are called spring, summer, autumn and winter. Each season is different.

In summer, the weather is often hot.
Plants bloom and animals grow.
The summer months are June, July
and August.

Summer weather

Summer is the hottest season of the year. The sun rises high in the sky. There may be storms, with thunder and lightning.

You always see lightning before you hear thunder.

Stay out of the sun in the middle of the day. This is when the sun is hottest. It is important to wear suncream when you are out.

Suncream will protect you from the sun's harmful rays.

Summer trees

In summer, many trees are covered with glossy green leaves. When the sun shines, the water in the leaves turns into a type of sugar. This sugar feeds the trees.

There is more sunshine in the summer than at any other time of year. This sunshine helps trees and plants to grow quickly.

When the sun shines brightly, it is cool and shady under a leafy tree.

Summer flowers

Plants need lots of sunshine for them to grow. Lots of flowers bloom in summer. Look out for beautiful sunflowers, roses and carnations.

Sunflowers always turn their heads to face the sun.

Insects drink a sugary liquid called nectar from flowers. As they feed, pollen sticks to them. The insects take pollen from plant to plant.

Pollen helps plants to grow again next year.

Animals in summer

Dragonflies take years to change from larvae into adults. Then they live for only a few weeks in summer.

Dragonflies lay their eggs under water.

You may be lucky enough to see snakes in summer, too. They bask in the sun to warm themselves. This gives them energy to catch prey.

Grass snakes are common in the UK.

Summer food

In summer, it is warm enough to eat outdoors. Picnics at the park or on the beach are great fun.

A picnic is a meal eaten outdoors.

Soft fruits like raspberries, cherries and strawberries are ripe and juicy. Ice lollies and ice cream are perfect for hot days.

There are thousands of flavours of ice cream. What is your favourite?

Summer holidays

Children have long school holidays in summer. There is lots of free time to play outside on bikes and scooters.

Riding a bike is an excellent way to stay fit.

Some people go on holiday. They may visit the seaside or stay at a campsite. Others travel on a boat or aeroplane to foreign countries.

At the beach, you can paddle, swim or just play in the sand.

Summer festivals

In the UK and the USA, summer is in the middle of the year. At this time of year, there are many music festivals to enjoy.

Hot, sunny weather is ideal for an outdoor festival.

In the USA, one of the most important festivals of the year is Independence Day. People celebrate Independence Day with parades, fireworks and concerts.

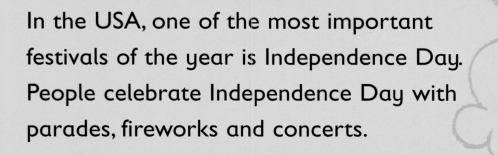

Independence Day is celebrated on 4 July in the USA.

Why do we have seasons?

We have seasons because Earth is tilted. As Earth moves around the Sun, different parts of the planet are nearer the Sun.

In **spring**, our part of the planet moves towards the Sun. The weather grows warmer.

In **summer**, our part of the planet is nearest the Sun. This means that the weather is hot.

In **autumn**, our part of the planet moves away from the Sun. The weather grows cooler.

In **winter**, our part of the planet is furthest from the Sun. This means that the weather is cold.

It takes a year for the four seasons
to happen. This is because it takes
a year for Earth to move around the Sun.

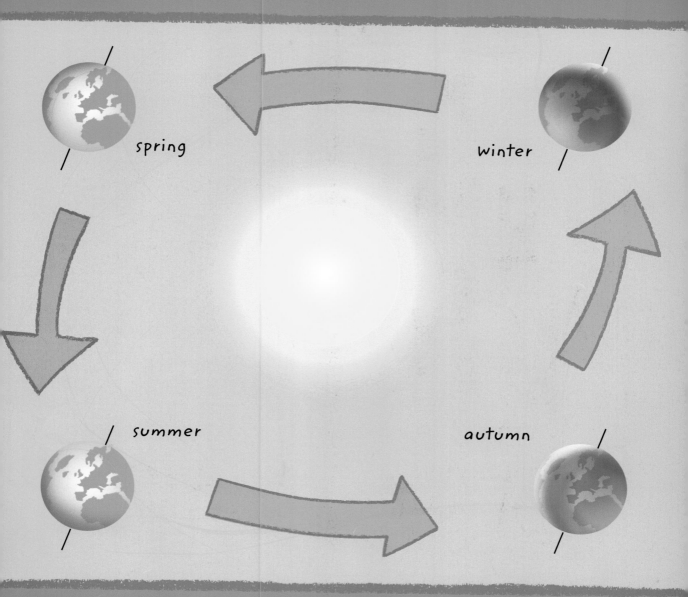

spring

winter

summer

autumn

Make a holiday scrapbook

Keep a record of the exciting things that happen in the summer holidays.

1. What did you do in the summer holidays? Where did you go? How did you get there? What did you see? Write it all down in your holiday scrapbook!

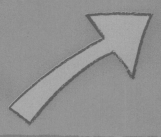

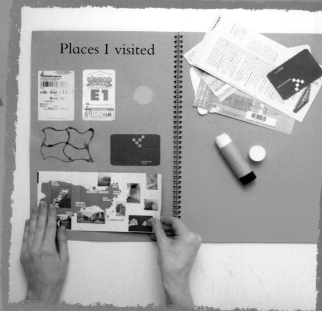

2. Collect leaflets and postcards from the places that you visit. Keep tickets of all kinds — bus tickets, boarding passes and tickets for the zoo. Then stick them all in.

3. Take photos and stick them in, too. Write place names beside the photos so that you always remember where you went.

4. You can keep it for ever. It will always remind you of summer!

Glossary

dragonflies brightly coloured insects that live near water

energy the strength to do something

foreign to do with another country

insect a tiny creature with six legs

larvae very young creatures

lightning bright light that flashes during a thunderstorm

nectar a sugary type of liquid that insects feed on

pollen powder found in flowers that is taken to other flowers by insects or blown there by the wind

prey animals that are hunted by other animals

thunder a loud noise that booms during a thunderstorm

Index

animals 5, 12–13

autumn 4, 20, 21

beach 17

Earth 20, 21

festivals 18–19

flowers 10–11

food 14–15

holiday 16–17, 20–21

insects 11

leaves 8

plants 5, 9, 11

spring 4, 20, 21

Sun 6, 7, 8, 9, 13, 20, 21

suncream 7

trees 8–9

weather 5, 6–7

winter 4, 20, 21